# Lucky

by Tim Hebert

Copyright 2013 by Tim Hebert.

All rights reserved. No part of this publication may be reproduced, distributed, or transmitted in any form or by an means, including photocopying, recording, or other electronic or mechanical methods, without the prior written permission of the author, except in the case of brief quotations embodied in critical reviews and certain other noncommercial uses permitted by copyright laws.

Printed in the United States of America on permanent paper.
Illustrated by Julie Leiman Weaver
Book design and production by Cindy Murphy, Bluemoon Graphics

ISBN: 978-0-9915789-0-0

The **Streaming Pen**™

West Greenwich, RI

*To my beautiful wife, Kim:
as luck would have it,
she made me the luckiest
person in the world.*

# Lucky

"Shhhh," said Grandfather.

"But, Po Po, you said you would read me another story," she said, almost in tears. It was hard to look into those hazel-colored eyes when water was beginning to form. A sniffle and a slight pout to her tiny lip was the deal clincher. Another story was on the way.

"Okay, Madison, but this is the last story for tonight." He tried to say this with some authority. But, Kim, his wife, was going to be upset; he'd been pushing himself all day long. He was tired, and he struggled to shake off his weariness for Madison's sake. "How's this one, about the big bad wolf?" he asked, holding up a book with torn pages and the ink worn out from the stress and strain of repeated readings.

Madison looked at him with those eyes and said, "You know that I don't like that one anymore, Po Po. Don't you have any new stories for me?" Now he was on the ropes. He'd read all of her favorite stories already.

Looking down on his granddaughter all tucked into her little Madison-bed, he wondered what he would do for the final go-to-bed story. Then, he had the most creative thought of the night: make up a story. He had a knack for telling stories. He was an expert at taking the small details of daily life and turning them into some grand adventure. His mind raced at the speed of thought searching for just the right idea, the right moment, the right story. An image of a small mouse from many years ago entered his consciousness and it took hold. That moment in his life seemed like a lifetime ago and so somber. He did not know why, but somehow it seemed appropriate on this night.

And now, as a seed of an idea started to grow, he became more alive. Every neuron in his brain fired in unison and conspired to pull this story to life. The more he thought about this moment, the more he desired to tell this particular story. He convinced himself that he could tell this story. It would take some work but he could do this! Now the greater task: convincing Madison that it was a good idea.

"Madison, we've read all of your favorite stories, and all we have left are the yucky stories that you don't like. But I will tell a wonderful story about your grandmother and me. I know you will like this story because it is about a cute little mouse named Lucky."

Madison looked at her grandfather with suspicious eyes.

"That's okay, Po Po, but tomorrow we better get some new stories." He almost burst out in laughter as the littlest boss spoke. 'God, she was just like her grandmother.'

Rubbing the fatigue from his eyes, he gathered his resolve. He said, "Yes, we'll get some new stories." He fumbled for a beginning. "Once upon a time…"

She looked at him quizzically. "Why do they all start with 'once upon a time'?"

At a loss for words, he nodded at her and then said, "Well, that's a good question. I guess that storytellers never know how to start a good story."

"Oh, are you a storyteller?"

"A poor one, honey," was his only reply. He knew this was going to be a long night.

"Anyway, it was a long time ago when I was younger. Kim and I went on a long trip far away from Rhode Island."

Before he could get another word out she questioned, "Who's Kim?"

With a chuckle he said, "Well, Madison, you know who Kim is; she is your grandmother, Mo Mo. We owned a little house in the woods in Maine. Our house in Maine was about four hundred miles from Rhode Island, a long, long way away. Our little place was magical, nestled in the middle of the woods, with no neighbors, except for the birds and bunny rabbits. We had to drive down a long dirt road to get to our cabin. Many times, we would see rabbits, squirrels, deer, and even moose as we drove down this dirt road."

"Moose!"

"Yes, big moose!" He lowered his voice to a whisper; he should be putting her to sleep, not getting her worked up with fantastical stories. Kim would be angry with him. He needed to take better care of himself. And as always, he had been pushing himself too hard. He could hear Kim telling him that he needed his rest and that he was not getting any younger, but it was what she didn't say that worried them the most. "Yes, Madison, big moose," he said with exaggerated arms thrown wide. "Some of these moose were seven feet tall, bigger than me, and they weighed more than a truck. They had huge antlers as big as your bed. They moved slowly, always watching you."

Barely breathing, Madison whispered, "Po Po, were you scared?" There was no greater pleasure in the world than watching a four-year-old engrossed. There was a simplistic beauty in her innocence and wonder. She would not sleep until this story was finished. He ran his tired fingers through his hair. The thinning got worse with each treatment. He would be bald soon. He was scared now.

"No, your grandmother and I loved the animals in our woods. Many animals came to greet us every time we came to visit, especially our friends the bunny rabbits. They loved your grandmother very much. She was always feeding them slices of bread.

"Did you know that bunnies loved bread?"

Her big eyes shined with amazement, as she shook her head with an overstated, "No!"

"Did the rabbits live in your house?" she asked.

"No, dear. They lived in their own little rabbit homes in the woods, but they did like to visit. On this special day, our two bunny friends, Peter and Paula, were there to greet us as we pulled up to our house. Peter's long ears twitched as he listened to us unload our truck, and Paula's nose wiggled in anticipation as she tried to smell if we had brought her any bread.

"Our house was the perfect place for us and our animal friends. We loved our house. Mo Mo would sit in front of our house feeding our friends as the smoke from the chimney rose through the trees that stood over us. Our little gray house looked like a barn with windows, sitting in the middle of the woods. Not far from our cabin was a river that provided soft music to put us to sleep at night. When we opened the door, we entered our shelter from the weather, but there was not much more. We didn't have electricity or water, but our house had all the comforts of home."

"Did you have a TV?" she asked.

"No. You need electricity for TV to work," he replied.

"What did you do with no TV?" she asked, puzzled.

"Your grandmother and I spent a lot of time talking. We spent lots of time reading stories. And we played games. Ssshhh," he said, leaning closer to her, "and never play backgammon with your grandmother, because she cheats!" He winked, bringing his right index finger to his mouth to signal their shared secret. Madison laughed, bringing both hands to her face. She was getting sleepier. Watching her, he longed to be young again, to be able to relive these moments again. He longed to experience the world with innocent eyes, to feel that sense of wonder at the slightest of details, and to truly appreciate the moment.

"Our house did not have much. Inside there was a wood stove that burned wood to keep us warm, and a stove to cook our meals. We had a table where we ate our meals and an old battered couch."

"Po Po, where did you sleep?"

"We slept in a very special place; we slept in the roof. We climbed up a ladder into the roof, where we had a small bedroom. This room was very tiny. I could not stand up without banging my head on the ceiling. There was a window in our bedroom, and from this window we could hear the birds sing their morning songs and the gentle rush of the river flowing past us. As we slept, we were surrounded by the forest and all of its creatures."

"But where would I sleep?" she wondered aloud.

"We have a special Madison-bedroom right next to ours, and from that window you could watch the bunny rabbits play. But, this trip was different; it was very special. After we unloaded the truck of all our clothes and our food, a curious movement caught my eye."

"Was it a bunny? Po Po, was it a bunny?" she squealed as she pulled her blanket to her lips.

"No, not a bunny, but something even more special!" he replied.

"It must be the mouse!" Madison said in the most adult voice she could muster.

"Not exactly, Madison. It was something even more precious. It was a baby mouse, maybe a couple of days old. It was lying right next to the front wheel of my truck. I missed running over the baby mouse by mere inches."

"A baby mouse?" Madison shrieked with joy.

"This mouse was very tiny, maybe as big as my thumb!" he said showing his thumb to her. Madison reached out and touched her grandfather's thumb in awe. "This baby mouse was struggling to move from its side to its feet, but it did not have the strength. I watched the mouse for several minutes; it was so young that its eyes hadn't opened yet. I ran into the house to get your grandmother. When your grandmother took one look at the baby mouse, she fell in love and began to cry."

"Why was Mo Mo crying?" Madison asked.

"She was afraid for the baby mouse because she knew that the mouse would die if it was left alone. But we were afraid to touch it, because some animals will not help their babies if people have touched them. So your grandmother and I decided to let the mouse stay outside for a while, to see if the baby's mother would rescue it."

"Did the mommy come?" Madison asked, almost in tears.

"Your grandmother and I waited for many hours for the mother to show, but she never did. Every five minutes your grandmother would stand up and stare out the window, waiting for the mother to rescue it. We waited and waited. The weather was getting bad; it got colder, and the wind blew hard. Every time the baby tried to get to its feet, along came the wind and knocked it to the ground.  As the weather grew worse and the daylight started to fail, the mouse lay on a cold stone slowly dying."

"No!" pleaded Madison as tears formed in her eyes. She was just like her grandmother.

"Finally, Mo Mo threw on her coat and ran to the baby. She picked up the poor, smaller-than-a-thumb mouse; it struggled to find shelter in her hands.  In the center of her palms lay the little mouse, barely breathing and occasionally issuing a high-pitched squeak. Your grandmother looked at me with tears in her eyes. 'We have to save him. We have to save Lucky.'

"Madison, the moment your grandmother picked up the tiny mouse she named him Lucky. She said that we were lucky to see him because he was so small. That he was lucky that we found him because it was very cold that day and we brought him into our warm house. Your grandmother and I knew that he was lucky to be alive."

He thought back, remembering how hard that year had been for Kim. She had spent the entire Thanksgiving and Christmas holiday season caring for her dying father. Every day began with new hope that he would survive but each night left her in tears. She felt as though his death in January was her failure. She could not beat death. Lucky had become her second chance. She wanted to prove, once and for all, that her father's death was not her fault.

"We placed Lucky into a small plastic container with one of your grandmother's socks for warmth and padding. We weren't prepared to care for a baby mouse. We got into our truck and drove to Farmington, the next big town. We needed supplies to save him. Farmington was less than an hour from our camp. For the entire trip, your grandmother hovered over him with his eyes still closed and she spoke soft, gentle words to him. We both knew that his time was running out."

"Po Po, Lucky didn't die, did he?" Madison cried. She was just like her grandmother. How could he tell her that Lucky had died and was buried behind the camp with pile of stones as his silent marker? Kim had failed to beat death; she failed to keep Lucky alive. He decided that he couldn't tell her.

"No, little one, Lucky did not die," he reassured her. "Mo Mo spoke softly to Lucky, holding his weak little body in the palm of her hand. She stroked his little head with her index finger. At the store, we bought some baby formula and an eyedropper, which we used to feed him. Without a mommy mouse to nurse him, we had to feed him from an eye dropper."

"I remember when mommy had to nurse Samuel, and as he got bigger she gave him a baby's bottle," Madison said.

"That is right!" he said. "The eyedropper was like a baby's bottle, but a lot smaller. Mo Mo held him in the palm of her left hand, while she used her right hand to feed him. On the drive, your grandmother attempted to feed him. It was hard to tell how much food he actually ate and how much was spilt on his face. But Mo Mo would not give up; she was going to do everything in her power to keep him alive. With his eye still closed and his ears folded back to his head, he had become her little child. And she was going to save his life.

"By the time we got home, your grandmother had fed Lucky enough food for him to sleep. He'd curled up into a tight little ball in her hand. His cute little paws with their miniature fingernails held his slender tail, which was longer than his entire little body. We watched Lucky for hours, marveling at his small features—his white nose, and white whiskers—and looked for signs of life.

"Then it was time to go to bed, because big people need their sleep, too," he sighed. "Your grandmother put Lucky into his plastic house." He could still remember the image of the lifeless mouse in Kim's blue eyes. That night she cried for Lucky and for her father. Now, Lucky needed her. He was depending on her and she would not fail him. She was battling for his little life. She was a fighter and she would not be going down without a fight.

He continued, "When the next day rose, your grandmother jumped out of bed and went to his container. She stood there waiting for his next breath, counting softly to herself: one-one thousand, two-one thousands, three-one thousands. Finally, she saw the gentle motions of his chest as he took one breath after another. Your grandmother cried tears of joy, for she knew that he survived the hardest part."

"Yay! Lucky lived!" exclaimed Madison.

"Sssshhh! We have to keep the noise down," he said lowering his voice. "Grandmother is nice to a little mouse but she is very mean to grandfathers who keep little girls awake by telling them stories."

"But, but, but what happened to Lucky?" she pleaded.

"He was touch and go for several days, but your grandmother nursed him back to perfect mouse health. She held him in one hand while he was on his back, and she held the eyedropper in the other hand. After a few moments, he would start nursing from the eyedropper.

Both eyes still closed, he held on to the eyedropper for dear life with both tiny mouse paws. Once the nursing started, he would use both paws to force the milk from the eyedropper.

"As Lucky grew stronger, he went with us everywhere. He would ride in the pocket of your grandmother's shirt. Every once in a while, he poked his snow-white nose and white whiskers out of her pocket to smell the air around them. After a week, his eyes opened and looked at your grandmother for the first time. His dark black pools for eyes looked deeply into her soul. If Mo Mo did not love this furry creature before, she was in love with him now. Soon his ears stood from the top of his head, and twitched to every sound around him."

"You're not telling another crazy story, are you Timothy?" Kim said in her most stern voice she could muster. She was standing in the doorway to Madison's room with her arms folded. "I thought you fell asleep while reading to Madison."

"No, I am just finishing a story," he stammered.

"Mo Mo, I want a mouse like Lucky!" exclaimed Madison.

Leveling her stern gaze upon her granddaughter, Kim said, "Young lady, aren't you supposed to be asleep by now?" She bit her lower lip as she held back her tears. "Now it is time for young girls and foolish old men to be in bed, sleeping."

"But, Mo Mo, what happened to Lucky?" Madison begged.

Looking at him, Grandmother said, "Go ahead, and finish your story, old man." She leaned against the doorframe as she listened to him finish his yarn about Lucky. But he could tell that she was not listening to his words.

"You see, Lucky was a wild mouse, and he needed to be back in the wild. On the day we released him, Mo Mo was very sad. She knew that Lucky must be set free, but she did not want to let go. After we placed him on the ground, he ran off a few feet from your grandmother and sniffed the air around. Tears streamed down your grandmother's face. After a few minutes of crying and whispered goodbyes, your grandmother and I retired to our camp. Through the window, we watched him playing in the yard. Then he disappeared and we did not see him for the rest of our stay."

"What happened to Lucky?" Madison persisted.

"Oh, get on with it, Timothy," Kim said. "Your grandfather has such a flair for the dramatic!"

He began to finish what he started, but it was not the flair for the dramatic that stopped him. It was hard to speak when his heart was in his throat. He knew that no matter how much Kim loved him, or how much she took care of him, or how many stories he told, he would die. The cancer was eating him away. The doctors told him to expect no more than a year. He wanted to believe in Lucky, but his luck was running out. He could, now and forever, change the mouse's luck. "As I said, we did not see Lucky again on that trip. But on our next trip to our camp he greeted us at the door, sitting on his hind legs playing with his long mouse-tail with his front paws, waiting for our arrival. Our mouse had grown up, but still he was not much bigger than my thumb. For the rest of the year, Lucky would stop and visit on our trips to our little house in the woods." Whether it was surprise or gratitude, Kim looked at him with those eyes that said thank you.

In reality they'd never made another trip back to Maine after Lucky died. They never spoke about it but they both knew it was more than a mouse that haunted her.

"Is that the end of the story, Po Po?" Madison asked through a small yawn. She raised her arm and brought the back of her hand to her mouth as she closed her eyes, falling to sleep.

"For now, little one, for now." He climbed from his chair and rose to meet his wife. As they embraced, tears streamed down her face, and she whispered, "Let's go to Rangeley next weekend." His gentle kiss on her cheek was his silent confirmation.

# Gratitude

I started writing this short story ten years ago, and for many years it was nothing more than a Microsoft Word file lost in some dusty and cobweb-infested folder on my computer. For many years, **Lucky** sat there untouched and unfinished. Waiting.

It took a lot courage and confidence to begin the expedition to rediscover this story and bring it to life. This journey began in mid-October 2013, when I shared my idea of creating a book as a Christmas gift for my wife with my friend Ken Lizotte. Ken gave me the confidence and courage that this could be done. And now, I am here writing the acknowledgement for a book that will soon be finished.

In high school, I was told by a teacher that I would never be a writer, that I simply was not good enough. Suffering from dyslexia and a short attention span, I believed her. When I started this journey, I was very self-conscious, the echoes of that teacher's voice and words ringing through my head. Elena Petricone and Fran

Harrington, your kind words and encouragement made those memories fade. I knew that I could be a writer and publish this story. Thank you for your sharp eyes, soft pens, and your tender guidance.

I am a visual person, and when I started writing this story it played through my head like an animated movie. I spent numerous hours trying to find the right words to bring the story to life. As the book project took shape, I wanted to include a visual element that played alongside the story. Illustrator Julie Leiman Weaver took on the project on short notice, with very little direction, and pressed by a tight timeline. Despite all that, she successfully created a beautiful visual element to my story.

During the development of this book, I had many ideas and wanted the book to have a certain look and feel. Because of pressing timelines, a small quantity of books, and limited resources, I had to make many sacrifices. Though the first printing will not have the desired cover or the interior paper quality that I had conceived, I refused to make compromises on the way I envisioned the words on the pages. My good friend, Keith Sereby, came to my rescue and provided guidance on font types and size. Without Keith's counsel, this book would have looked like any other book.

I once read this quote: "Gratitude is the memory of the heart." For all those that joined my journey to publish **Lucky**, you will always be a memory in my heart. Thank you!

# Author Biography

You have never met anyone like him. Highly-energized, compassionate, ingenious, and just plain "awesome," Oscar T. Hebert is a visionary and a leader. With a personal mission to light a fire in the hearts and minds of those around him, Tim truly impacts lives. As Atrion's CEO, President, Captain, and Superhero, Tim has driven himself and Atrion over the last twenty years to remain on the cutting edge of the IT services industry so as to propel Atrion to become a top 1% organization. In that effort, he and Atrion have been successful.

But Tim's passion for people, leadership, and relationships extends far beyond merely leading his Atrion family into success and growth.

Tim believes that there is more to business than simply "turning a profit," and that every business should be driven by purpose and core values. He has infused Atrion with its core purpose of "having a positive impact on the lives of others," which has created a dynamic culture and made Atrion one of the best places to work. An influential role model, Tim has taken leadership roles within the community too, as a Year-Up mentor, a Trustee for the Rhode Island Public Expenditure Council, a Director of the Rhode Island Economic Development Corporation, and even as the President and Chairman of the non-profit organization Tech Collective.

**Lucky** is Tim's first published work of short fiction. It was started a decade ago and remained relatively untouched until the fall of 2013 when it was resurrected as a personalized Christmas gift for his wife Kim, the inspiration for the book's story.

Tim and Kim reside in West Greenwich, Rhode Island with their three dogs—Maxie, Rogue, and Storm.

Printed in the USA
CPSIA information can be obtained
at www.ICGtesting.com
LVHW070910041023
760083LV00004B/145